SIDEBROW BOOKS

On Wonderland & Waste

On Wonderland & Waste

SANDY FLORIAN

Collages by Alexis Anne Mackenzie

SIDEBROW BOOKS • 2010 • SAN FRANCISCO

Published by Sidebrow Books
912 Cole St., #162
San Francisco, CA 94117
sidebrow@sidebrow.net
www.sidebrow.net

Cover art ("Thorax Vulture") by Alexis Anne Mackenzie
Cover & book design by Jason Snyder

ISBN: 0-9814975-1-9
ISBN-13: 978-0-9814975-1-8

FIRST EDITION | FIRST PRINTING
9 8 7 6 5 4 3 2 1
SIDEBROW BOOKS 002
PRINTED IN CANADA

Sidebrow Books titles are distributed by
Small Press Distribution

Titles are available directly from Sidebrow at
www.sidebrow.net/books

A Member of
inter
section
incubator
Services for Artists
www.theintersection.org

Sidebrow is a member of the Intersection Incubator, a program of
Intersection for the Arts (www.theintersection.org) providing fiscal
sponsorship, networking, and consulting for artists. Contributions and
gifts to Sidebrow are tax-deductible to the extent allowed by law.

Grateful acknowledgment to the editors of the following publications, in which pieces from this book first appeared:

bird dog: "The Tree of No"
Coconut: "The Muffles of Dolls"
Deconstruction: "Dumb Show & Noise"
Diagram: "On Dissecting the Body & Lumber"
Horse Less Press: "Franchise"
identity theory & *Elixir Magazine*: "Postscript"
Sidebrow: "And Your Messages"
Sleepingfish: "Double-Bolted Doors"
Tammy: "How the Clouds Hung" & "Swimming the Elephants"

"Franchise" was written in collaboration with DZ Delgado.

On Wonderland & Waste

The Tree of No

Beastly, I fall at Adam under the shade, unclocked, first frocked, ovened at the core, from words no western man can wet. Beastly, I fall at Adam under the shade, shaking shadows from the shadows, pretending, beastly, that toads aboard the oncoming train are throned, green toads of the goodliest worth. Beastly, debarred, hunted, wanton, I take refuge by the timber, entrapped in the awkward position of wanting.

The high hitch of increase sways softly in the sun, here in our scarlet garden, grounded by growth and considerable in size. This is our forest full of fairies. Slanted and pendant without verb or vowel. Like an herbivored perfumery. An arboreal experiment. An intricate system of soil and seed. Where the wind knocks down pippins and greenings.

Beastly, I, with crooked teeth, stand under the crooked tray, muttering to myself to kill or be spilled. Beastly, I, with blistered fingers, fit to stand, fit to fall, unhesitate to taste the waste. Beastly and with blistered fingers, I bear the bone from the blossom, pare the pleasures off the round, taste, for the first time, the adamantine sublimity, nine times the measure of day and night.

Gold grows under the majesty of roses. Every elegance is a governmental factor. My wound is also washed by wonder. And it is now, that I begin to fall in love with Montgomery.

Beastly, I, replete and eaten, sever the trunks to count the cocoons, one-one-thousand, two-one-thousand, weltering in the power of my consummate crime, like the yellower edges of guiltier graves. Time becomes my deputy. Time becomes my authority. As extended from the single. Signaling a system. The royal trunk has left a circumference. And it's now that I begin to fall in love with Montgomery, celestial standing under branches waving. That perennial plant having wood.

My fair faith is foul. My fair faith is feigned. In my pressed heart, my fair love blanches with pronunciation. Leaves and petals now bend down. Downtrodden with our migration.

What a pull, I think. Lie in bed, I think. I will be as lame as a muscle, I think. You will be wanting some yourself come dinner time. I am thinking, in a rational manner, of poles planted in liberty. Flags floating for democracy. I am thinking of emancipation. Of law. Of the newfound independence to franchise our freedom. We will live in the narrative garden. Yielding oil. That curious alchemical experiment.

What a yank, I say, you may be uncomfortable now, but I will not let you die in their polychromatic prayers. See, the green grass flows upon molehills. Besides, we will have mercy on Adam and send him out to the angels. Our bigness will come in clusters. Our bigness will come in orchards. Our bigness will come in vessels, hermetically sealed and siphoned.

If you press me to tell you why I love him, I feel that reason itself cannot be expressed. I can only echo. Because it is he. Because it is I. Because it is he. Because it is I.

Beastly, I make bed of it. A convict, plump and stumbling trunk of it. Avenue, beltway, tube, and brick of it. Hut and house of steer and steel. I am big in a general way. Though my enchanter is far fancier than the planter. Instrumental in my overarched endeavors. I am tangling myself, like a locomotive, feeding. I am shaking myself, like a locomotive, feeling. I am building the surfeit city. From the farming and the felling.

It's Christmas at the introduction to Our Father who art in heaven. The trio we plant in the tub. Bow between bough and bark. One part of the structure, like a sinking ship. The second element in combination. Bridges we lay for the conveyance of sorrow. Then, there's Watson under the wire. A singing bird upon the mast. A damned dame gurgling under the wood. Waxing under the stellar moon.

The moon we call Diana. Goddess of our broken grove. Whereby the mixture of silver, quick-silver, and spirit may be codified into the right form. Passing time we call Saturn and record it with a monkish chronography. Rainbow belts around the rainbow belly. Crystal we call the nervous system. Consisting of cords and organs forking. Stemming loud from the braided brain. Like a hierarchical network of finite numbers. On a terminal street. Then, with the use of a pistol and a linguist, we select from the phrases, and store them with a cuff link and a candle.

It's Christmas at the introduction to Our Father who art in heaven. Speech we bury in the garden. Rope between bark and bark. One part of the structure, like a maze. Bridges we lay for the conveyance of rain. Then, there's Watson under the wire. A burning bird inside the nest. A damned dame gurgling under the cross, pebbling her polychromatic prayers.

The hero is the volitional ego that chooses. The plot is a succession of time. The time I choose to portray is arbitrary. As the passing of time to death is but a necessity.

So today I was busy with Montgomery about planting on the bend of Greenbelt between I-95 and 270. He refused to contribute to the fund. So I set him down at the root to comfort him. I told him about the place he loved, covered in concrete fields and amply shaded by skyscraper fliers. He listened, silent as the shadows. Charming, really. Then he became aware of the problem and lay himself supine in the treebox. He planted a seed and started naming the daisies: amaranth, cabbage, carnation, willow, fuchsia, houseleek, mallow, melon, primrose, mignonette, rhododendron, pea, violet, poppy, wormwood, azalea, boxwood, barbata, cactus, lily, creeper, clover, cotton, cranberry, peony, olearia, konini, germander, heath, lotus, nettle, lucerne, lungwort, onion, orchid, lupine, poke, purslane, sorrel, sassafras, chestnut. All of those that fringe the fettered fen. I indulged him with a visit to the she-box where a she-bird lay sleeping on a she-fork. He took a bite of the ten-thousand-headed cabbage. One-one-thousand, two-one-thousand. While I took a bite of a mummy. Together we turned the well-wooded garden into graveyards.

On this page filled with mere words, I will also report a dream. I was sitting at the edge of a kidney-shaped lake. I thought to myself, *Where?* then, *Who?* But I did not have the faculties of resolve. Sensing that my solitude had been intruded, I called out and heard a sharp reply. I looked around seeing no one but myself. So again I called out, and again I heard the sharp reply. My fear grew with the rustling of leaves. Then I thought to myself, this desolate awakening is infernal. This eternal echo is my destiny.

My prosthetic leg made from wood. See me crippled under the crippled trunk. Under a cloud of witnesses. All chopped.

As a sculptor, I choose the best spot to hang myself. The empty space around the dangle, I fill with grotesqueries and idleness. Then I wondered to myself. What are these feelings of mine, but monsters, or bodies, pieced together anaphorically? What are these feelings of mine but divers without order or proportion?

From fuller heights I begin to fall in love with Montgomery, supine in the treebox, half-drowned and making sounds: ant, bee, kangaroo, boa, beetle, partridge, linnet, monkey, slug, chafer, cuckoo, falcon, worm, shrike, squirrel, swallow, pipit, wasp, butterfly, raccoon, fox, cricket, crow, pigeon, dove, duck, finch, sparrow, fish, fly, hopper, lizard, lobster, cicada, aphis, martin, mouse, oyster, porcupine, runner, crab, spider. Squirrel of arboreal habits, as distinguished from a ground, tiger, warbler, frog, toad. It was then. It is now. I begin.

I am building the surfeit city from agate and dentils. I hire pruners and loggers who use chainsaws and tweezers. Across the crooked streams I lay fellings for the conveyance of sorrow. Trunks I carve for the calamities of death. Then, I contract the qualified carpenter. For it is a custom among my people to build our habits between the branches. We prop the ladders against the trunks and assemble them. Like nests. Then we fill our houses with ammunition and a rosary.

We claim the property with taxation and a number. And fix it by proportion and history. Then we pray for security against lightning and thunder. We burn sap for the repellence of static.

We furnish them with circles and squares. We furnish them with electricity and clocks. Then we put in fall fronts and pigeonholes. Inside the holes, we store our feelings and experiences according to size and proportion. We build boxes. Lots of boxes. Then we build bomb shelters and prisons. We learn agriculture and husbandry. Then we toss a gate across a public road and call it culture.

Iron we use to connect to doubles. The latter to the tongue of trucks. Hooks and clips by which to trace. Naked boulders over naked molehills.

To dare the broken bridge across the stream, I draw a diagram of a sentence. In the diagram, only the configuration matters. Not the length of the spectacle. Then, I make a hollow booming for the drumming. And, when I am high and dry, I climb the ladder to my house. Shoot the spectacles from the doubling. Language facilitates in the field of listening. That oaky operation of trebbling.

In the beginning, there was a beetle, blind as a bat, whispering vulgarities at the door. Then there was the butterfly, broadly thoraxed and rigidly tongued. He communicated ghosts from a stringed-up wing. Then god said, let there be leeches, and they became plentiful in the forest. Then god said, let there be snakes, and they became a sad drawback to the pleasures of hunting. Then god said, let there be wasps, tarantulas, scorpions, stingrays, piranhas, and Mexican bearded lizards.

We play pin the coconut on the pine tree. He puts me in a fix. Drives me up a tree. Narrows me in the trenches. Like a hunted animal. A wild beast. While I am barking up the wrong tree. Because it's no use. I have no security. After all, I am imagining myself swing-like. Dangling from the unadorned branch.

The earliest sense goes with the original sense, but the word was soon laid down to supply the noun. Be it acknowledgment or confession. Many barns also barn. Without space. To impart. The napkin scam we made dominion over sac. But that was for my sake. That was for my shame. Nothing had been made by me, ever. Neither the pools in Liverpool, nor those things that might not lawfully have been made gods. For every nugget there is a dram of gold. For every wooden wheel there is a great brigade. That's what makes superiority an influence.

I catch sight of Joseph erect in his secret. He is muttering with Montgomery about the enemy. He is a deformed linguist disguised in a threadbare cloak. Struggles to keep them in the no. In Amsterdam he wears colors and sallies out to soldiers. Says he's been with Jesus in a judicial kind of inquiry. That little man with his mechanical indiscretions. Justice takes the officers by the government. Paul appeals to be freed. Liberty is postponed until the end of the war. It's then that I fall in love with Montgomery, over and over again. Marooned by the mirrors in his crown-shaped eyes. But his status is not gratis and so I hear out the merchants who have not been the same since. They have letters. Lots of letters. And they convey them by slave over the sorrowful bridges. I, for one, have never been one for whores. Chores, scores, bores. It's the pedestal itself I adore.

He, of course, is all bounteous and liberty to acquaintance. I want to be loved and so fall into seasons. Rote by rote, I marry the corporal to the cognate. The criminal to the carnal. Unabided by and by. From branches to branches. Clouds to clouds.

The object of the mind is only implied, but it helps all the same. So, civil wars are equated with ascension. Mining with darkness and obscurity. You can make a big deal from the principles of augury. And it makes me think, I think. I would like to go for a walk, I think. I would like to warble a hymn, I think.

I might be laboring in obscurity by the eerie acknowledgment of toadies. So, I can call upon the hour to recognize my study.

According to the measure and proportion of law, I keep five fat Franciscan friars in the furnace. A lovely woman tapers off into a fish.

Last night, I awoke under the full orbed moon, like a dazzling dare, a dampish dream, a phantom guest, a broken stream, as the rounded earth with balanced air battled at the beam.

We speak of books. We speak of symbols. We speak of poetry. We speak of night. Every number is abstracted from the number. Marks begin to multiply. To signal out the system. Unlanding the landing. Of caskets. Of factories. Of industries. Plants of the goodliest worth. Bearing wood.

I am building the surfeit city. I hire scientists and mathematicians and computer technicians. Bridges I lay for the conveyance of sin. Then I contract the qualified carpenter. For it is customary to build our habits between the branches. Like nests of the cormorant birds. But there is a line above which we cannot grow. With reference to altitude and latitude. There it only snows in rows. Marble banks against the broken ozone.

The planner is constructing an apprentice for the program. Computers are based on process and drive. The word can now be doubted as. When all these odds are fairly ended, my box is securely stored.

The next day, of course, we visit the factory. The teacher asks if I have ever seen a school. I organize a protest and find myself headed for the presidency. We are being trained for managers and technocrats. Hierarchy having the correct effect of lingering. The question was, the question is, how to organize a system that makes a god?

But this is ambiguous and so I will clarify. Last night I dreamt of a lake. It seemed to me another awkward sky. I looked inside the lake and saw my own face mirrored back at me drowning.

But this is ambiguous and so I will clarify. Last night I had a dream. I was flying through the sky like an angel, like a devil, and I kept saying the words, *I love, I love*, like a skywriter, a highflier, a falling shooting star. But the words kept dropping like bombs upon the opaque globe.

But this is ambiguous and so I will clarify. Last night I dreamt of a lake on fire. A lovely woman tapered off into a fish. A better paid witness might have preferred a peacock.

I zoom out to gain a perspective.

The production of ideas is a socially useful labor power. Our institutions ensnare us by algebra. After all, if *x* can equal anything, pathologies are certain to grow in the inner ear.

It can hardly be doubted that nouns have a common origin. What this means is not easy to determine. There is no parallel in action. Some relate it to wedlock. But neither Montgomery nor I can find the trace nor the train.

It has been proposed to associate action with tension as they were born at the same time. Adjectives stand in for relation. Like an ethnic cul-de-sac. Like a dead end. A blind alley. Or a standstill. We are supposed to stand about being treated like tigers. But instead, we, beastly, and with blistered fingers pare the pleasure from the plums. Tasting, for the first time, the unhesitating waste. Falling, for the first time, in love.

Parallel to this on the other side is the distinction between acquaintance and delineation. So, I may say, *I know, I know*, and by that fact relate a condition. Formerly a faculty of my confession. The mind is a place not immediately there. As location, it suffers from the repugnance of ideas to ideas.

So, shut the door is a limit to the mind. That's a sign that bears a sign. This is the argument that makes me happier, if, in fact, the door were etched in my memory. As it stands, the door is just a stump in the country.

The futile do forget, in feebleness of fancy. This is not Montgomery's opinion. But the opinion of the pure. He brings me belief between truth and severity. Now consisting. In extension. From the cause to the clause. After all, he is in the production of names. He is in the production of production. While Adam's all on cloud nine. Stuck in the muck and done by thunder.

The ignorant city in my king where folks scurry to make mistakes. Mariners we understand by their practicality. The art is more scarce than the dollar.

The negative prides itself on the negative. Wisdom is humble in its maze. I publish with a kind of declaration. That I am made from the matter of mothers. I am made from the matter of matter. I may publish the shape of a continent the same way I publish the shape of summation. To add is to compute. To compute is to comprehend. To comprehend is King. This is my ignorant city.

My big city is a city of big bombs and bicycles. My big city is a city in which the revelations are not revelations, but the precious portents of power. Someone throws the body overboard. The hero is the volitional ego that chooses. The plot is a succession of time. The time portrayed is arbitrary. As the passing of time to death.

My surfeit city is open to severality. Like the underwater underworld. Or an offshore engineer undergoing a subsea construction. Viscous. Fruitful. Deflowered. By the rigs of a drill ship. Factors being the average number of alternatives.

What a melt, I think. What a precursor to the father, I think. I am hanging myself from the mouth. I am thinking, in a rational manner, of the climb. And it's now that I begin to fall in love with Montgomery. Doubled in his dilated eyes.

Beastly, I climb the taller line thinking the intelligent perennial would be largely unmoving. There is a subtle numbness in my right leg. I strive to put the pruning to the test. Computation by computation, I am striving to become an astronaut. I am working toward making rockets from her stately rings. So I climb the line, higher and higher, until I fall, beastly, stony, wilted, withered, boxy, bony, eaten. Representing the yellower form of treason. I am not a spirit in the practice of worship. My jack-in-the-box is the humiliating embodiment.

If you press me to tell you why I love him, I feel that reason itself cannot be expressed. I can only echo. Because a father hurls a son off a high cliff and hangs.

Fuller heights from fall to fall. It wasn't soon before the felling. It wasn't soon before the asking. How did we achieve this pit? How did we achieve this abyss? For every green plum that falls from the sky, another star in heaven. For every clap. For every bolt. We are dropping down from rooftops. Fixing our feet in the sorrow. Like every inch of hail. Like every mount of snow. It's the number of the meteors that matter. It's the number of challengers that matter. Phantom falls of the phantom hounds. Love is so voluble and sunken. It's the eyes that smear. Like a tossing of rain over unspent sand. Like a dropping of teeth from the hollow mouth. Like the symmetrical fall shoulders. A honeyed tongue. A heart of gall. The setting of the wider sun. I stand in the narrative garden. Holding its corpse by relation. I stand in the dawn of darkness. Where echoes fall from utterance. Mortal sorrows sing the melody divine. One man hangs himself. Slain by the sound of words. Swiping the ground to meet the ball rolling. Now we wrestle with all kinds of creatures. So let a fish come so that I may fall. Let the fowl come so that I may follow. Let me lapse by the unswerving glass. In the end, it's all endings always. In the end, it's all stones and doorways. In the end, I begin.

To approach the right light in spring. To sunbathe in the summer. To make coats woven from winter and ultrasuede. In the autumn, I see the comet catastrophe. Shooting between the words, *Let there be*, and, *There is*. That is the local apocalypse. Presented by the universal blank.

Between creativity and creation there lies a calamity. So I may say, *Let there be love*, and in saying so, I imagine it and make it live.

It's Christmas at the introduction to Our Father who art in heaven. The trio we plant in the sink. Fist between popcorn and tinsel. Hollow balls we hang at the end of the branches to represent fruit. That pretty metallic vegetation. The presents we wrap in parcels and plant them in the shade. Then we call upon the children with their crystalline curiosities, little boys with their waxen wings. Because it's the children who fall and fall.

I am learning the streets of this new city. I live here who loves my pain. With my yellow pencil in my yellow taxi I draft a brotherly Order and his sister, Melancholy. I undertake the English Epic and puzzle over its broadways and bridges. Then, I borrow money. Month after month. And study with my yellowing reason to pass the examination. I quote the Russian because I know, yes, *I know*, that two plus two equals five.

It's Christmas at the introduction to Our Father who adores all kings and their kindly crimes. Now every grounded rock has been untangled. Now every tongue in charge can take a hand to lend a hanging. Tall, dark, dangling line. Now every tongue in charge can build a horse at the siege of Troy. A coffin with etchings of paisley. A cask of amontillado. The price of a gallon, five times three. One-one-thousand. Two-one-thousand. We are saddling the narrow now. Elliptical spring seat paddle. Block upon boot, we are busying ourselves with the branches, building the surfeit city. Paring our pleasures by the pendulum. See here. This is the root. That is our family vanity.

Last year, I was deleted without grace in Rome, Athens, Madrid, Paris, London, St. Petersburg, Caracas, Bogotá, Mexico City, Tokyo, Hong Kong, Buenos Aires, Vienna, Brussels, Sarajevo, Sofia, Ottowa, San José, Prague, Copenhagen, Santo Domingo, Quito, Cairo, Havana, Georgetown, Berlin, Baghdad, Dublin, Kuwait, Morovia, Oslo, Rabat, Panama City, Lima, Lisbon, Damascas, Bangkok, Tunis, Hanoi, Kingstown, Ankara, Managua, Warsaw, Maputo, Beirut, Amman, and Washington, D.C. Then, there's Adam groping paradise for the marmalade.

There is a little irregular square with Eden its hub. There, a muzzled dog, chained, runs circles around the rabid tree. Thus, although we cannot live, we are bothered by talking.

A winged and wilted boy falls from high in the sky. A lovely woman tapers off into a fish. Thus, although I cannot live here, I am bothered by reason.

In the beginning, god said, let there be hurricanes and tidal waves and earthquakes. In the beginning, god said, let there be typhoons and cyclones. God said, let there be volcanoes and let them be victorious. Let there be tornadoes and let there be famines and let them ravage man and his mind. Let there be pandemics, disease, pestilence, and poverty. Let there be science and let it be faulty. Let man be confused. Then god said, let man fear man and let man fear me. And with that fear, let there be holocausts and war. Let there be bombs and let them be atomic. Then god said, let there be wars. World wars. And there were wars. And god saw the wars. And they were good.

As I depart, I ought to make knowledge that I have been here. Rubbing two sticks between my fists, kindling a different kind of mystery. I am countering the foundation that underlies the city. Ambling through the bramble. Through the forest with a fire. Sticks between my fists. Assembling explosion.

Dumb Show & Noise

Hushed at the heart, unfolding the underwater O, I unfold myself to better understand your calamity. A piece of myself. This push between brow and brain. A clown stands on the scaffolding. The writing on the backwards wall says: On. On. You are the doctor of divinity. The doll of Denmark. Day between night and night. But hush. There is a ghost. There is a ghost that is not a ghost. That's where it all begins.

Have you relieved Horatio? A piece of him. Like the apparition between approving appearances. Let me assail your inner ear. Let me assail your tale. Here, when the nights are seen. Now, between down and down. These five minutes unfold in the sidereal skies that illuminate your piece of heaven. Your horrible heart. The doll of Denmark may be dying but I'm certain I could use a speech. So, speak if you have sound. So, pulse if you have heart. Quake yourself gently upon the opaque globe. So that I may forgive myself the offense of wonder. My gross and scoping fear.

There is a good eruption and you tell me what I want to know. You advise me to undergo a mathematical subdivision, so I revise myself: No. No. It is not like this world to go to war. It is not like this ship to sink. I go to the theater to watch myself on the watch. Like a sealed contract of ratified heraldry. Like an officer of arms without hand or hands. Like the man in the hamlet without mettle or bone.

With skill, I blow up the blundering balloons. Sinking in the forward scroll of it. All rolled up and ready to glow. This mote is more trouble to the mind's eye. In its high and blimey state. In its witchery and wisdom. If anything good could become, it has been suggested that we sheet the graves. With poly-cotton flowers. With pearl and sapphire blooms.

The dead squeak and the stars train and the blood disasters in the sun. A prologue to the omen. A moist star whose influence is empire, like a harbinger of the hitting. Like an influence on the outer shell. Like an absence of illumination. There is a ghost, so have you relieved in pieces? Stay, illusion. Take the play with paradox and abandon the examinations. I'd rather be drowning dumb than sedentary on your stage-fright stage. I'd rather be crowning now.

Soft, my wormy womb. Soft, my inconvenience. Soft, my gelatin and melting self. O. Like the underground corpse all trammeled and chested.

Soft, that dumb sparrow. Soft, this dumb sentence. Dropped from the dirge of marriage and vomiting the violets.

Winds give a benefit to my slumber. Ripples in the hush and silence. With a muffle and a mute, I cry, O, and O, sinking in my soft soliloquy, my soft and thorny road to heaven. You say I speak like a green girl. Unsifted but not untender. That I have importuned in my probable fashion. Then you say you love me and it is in my wisdom to believe it.

Love downs, between nouns and nouns, these hoops even I must leap. My words are not sterling, so I tender my tongue. Say it to stay, illusion, so I can fix my sodden eyes. I remember the acts in pieces. My mind is a place not entirely there.

A flourish of trumpets. Two shots and a drum. Blazes on the A-frame in the upside-down living room. Over the summit, a beetle. Over the sovereignty of reason. Over the fireplace, a put toy, without man or motive, some unfathomable brain. I hear the roar, holding my hands. I hear the heavy revel of the west. Reminding you to remember me. To sleep in the orchard where the serpent stings. Sleep, you who wears a crown. You whose eternity blazes. You whose head stays drunk on the pillow. Like the slightest word. Like the whirling sea. Your horrible sentence. Having witchcraft wits.

I who have fallen sink. In the deep blue sea. What is the shape of your sidereal sky? Between shifts, time stops on the half-side.

But this is ambiguous so I will clarify. I was sewing in my closet, I remember, when I heard. A nod, a now. Another noun. Carrying the stamp of defect. Glimpses of the moon waxing like so many fathoms. Deep in the deep. Then, the wherefore? The what should I? Followed by a question mark. Then I followed your questionable shape underwater. O. There I asked you to please.

There, there, I asked you to make. Make a ghost of my bony quake. Make a ghost of my joints and let me be. Make my eyes two startling fish, my marble jaws speak beyond this reach. Beetles on the base of this horrible delusion. Make me the toy poet of your desperations.

I followed your questionable further, longer, just beyond the rot. All the way to your celestial bed. The swift quicksilver alloys of my soft, my toy, my bone. O. These droppings of milk. Laser-like with embellished edges. Embellished by the opal blossom. Bosom-like with bested rest. Leave me to the instant old. Distracted by the other tone. Are you there, truepenny? Cankered by another mole?

We follow this question, but we never dreamt of philosophy, did we? Wondrous in its encumbered phrases. We never pronounced the sound and we never, through this ambiguous wood, wandered. Time is so out of joint. Marrying its rank companion. Noted by the statue standing out at sea. She is green in her dumbfound land. She is green in her demands. In her drift she wears the face of youth. And we see her, we, there, unfolding the underwater O, bubbling faintly in the shallows. These are the gallows of liberty. The taints of the furling minds. Unfetched by wit, unfetched by witness. Dreaming her philosophy by the gallons.

Observe the inclination to hang yourself.

I was sewing in my closet, I remember, knees knocking so pitiful and so profound. You suppressed the levies. I was ill at the numbers and it was my art, my heart. You placed on the coffee table my part, my mute and dumb. My light, my declination. My excellence of honor. Dead dogs on a dead end. Now I walk crabwise to the hole you dig.

My dream is not a shadow. Upon it, I cannot reason. There is a ghost, poor in thanks. There is a canopy overhanging. There is a majestic roof of gold and fire. Nothing approaches like a vat of vapors. There I go again, vomiting the venom.

The stage erupts in a pendulum of circumstance. A critic in the front row develops a theory of disarticulation. Then, the applause. Then, the performance of the applause. Someone calls it comedy. Someone calls it tragedy. But I know it is just a paragon of animals. Played by a paragon of angels. I know a hawk from a handsaw. A happy fool from his dumb gold. Two flies stuck on a pane: Buzz. Buzz.

An ominous horse, a paramour, a slope through the window, a slanting. The bold wind is speechless. A blanketing alarm of fear. This is the one-eyed lie. This is the one-eyed war. The bowl on the edge is bulging and I am sinking in my sinking ship. Ditto in my broken soliloquy. There, let me be ghostly. There, there, like the gauze-like epitaph of the ill report.

Have you relieved in pieces? Speak to me a dozen or some sixteen lines. Down the stage with your painted speech. Now between down and down, as the water-color nighttime widens. Be time. To my discretion tutor. Tear the word from this terrible observance. If I held a mirror to my nature, beastly, bony, wilted, eaten. If I held a mirror to my nature, half-drowned and making sounds. If I held a mirror to myself, that clown would settle down and make speeches. He is the necessary hybrid. That thump and drum of firefly swallow.

I think of nothing and that's a fair thought, unfolding the underwater O, but who? You've not yet forgotten though your hobbyhorse is long gone. I think of nothing and I speak what I think. These slender accidents, anchoring the blanks, discoursing the most elegant edges, the lowest notes on the top of my crowning compass. Here, in this little organ piping on the pipe. Here, by my little weasel, my weasel, my little whale. I will come by and by. When time stops on the half-side, tossing off its worser part.

One word, a worse one. Wanton on your drunken trunk. A mouse trapped in the mousetrap. A toad, a bat, a cat. Heaven cries, "A rat," for not understanding our love. My body is with me, but I am not within my body. Even on the eggshell. So, at supper, you eat where I am eaten. Your motherfather. Your fathermother. The huggermugger that inters me.

I am divided from myself, and that is a fair judgment. I hang underwater, and that's a fair thing. The doors are all broken and antiquity has been forgotten. Sinking now. A down. A clown. O, how the wheel becomes me. See? Fortune is the steward of my obscure funeral.

While you lie, head drunk on the bunk and sunk, sinking in my soft soliloquy made of this stuff so flat and dull. You like drowning my weedy trophies in the weeping brook. If I had a speech, I'd fain a fire. So, I ask you again to follow me to the unnumbered pearls, numbered by the looking glass gallows. With love.

Mornings

I sprained my ankle. I sprained the ankle of my right foot. It caused a straining, a sharp enduring pain. A lasting pain. A sprain.

I sprained the ankle of my right foot.

I say it repeatedly like a spoiled child. Over and over again, as if the episode materializes only at the time of its announcement. Before the announcement, and afterwards, the ankle is not sprained. The ankle would not matter. I would not exist.

I awoke one morning on the other side of town in a strange bed. It had lumps, fell deeper on one side than on the other. I slept on the incline, the side that slopes, so I could sleep satisfactorily only in the fetal position. Sleeping like a corpse would have sent me rolling to my left. Blue cotton sheets and a thin blue blanket. The smell of alcohol with a smoky stale stench.

A chill passed through me. I was cold in my sleep on the other side of town.

I awoke one morning in a strange bed. An alarm had rung. I rolled over, then over again. My body ached. I heard the sound of a television in the distance. Jesus was preaching. My eyes, half-open, half-shut, peered at the time. At the window. At the postcards on the bed frame. A blue postcard. A woman. Where have I seen that image before? The pendulum swung me to the left and I dreamt of a timeless place. Of the sounds of crashing water. And the smell of burning trees. A distant shatter. Children screaming, mothers scolding, "Get away from there!"

The pendulum swung eight minutes later with the mechanical sound of another alarm. The same alarm. The treasures of modern machinery and the "Five more minutes. I mean it, this time. Really." Only pleading is unnecessary. And time goes by faster.

I rolled over and scratched the back of the stranger lying next to me. A groan emerged from the chasms of his cryptic dream. His body trembled, briefly. Another chill. My own.

"Johnnie, Jesus is preaching. Don't you have to be somewhere?"

I heard the arousal of sound waves behind eye sockets light-years away. Sounds of an old Bug on a cold winter morning. Rusted. And bent. Like a jukebox in disguise repeating the same old American song. There was static. Jesus was preaching. My eyes, open, peered at the clock on the wall.

Time had passed. A relative issue.

We dressed and walked hand in hand toward the neighborhood coffee shop. We walked leisurely this time. The previous night we had walked quickly to a neighborhood bar. To the bar with the cow on the corner. A bar we had been to before, a few times on Saturday nights. This Saturday night, we walked closer together, arm in arm like newly found lovers in a black-and-white postcard. We talked about the stars and their sounds. The planets. The galaxies. The sun and its metallic brilliance. We wondered what sounds Earth made. And how we could record it.

At some point that night, I was told I was walking too fast, I was instructed to slow down. "You're always in a hurry to get somewhere," he said. The voice sounded strange. Displaced. Metallic, even. Thoughtful, perhaps, of a long lost love. Some people should marry their first love. Otherwise they spend their lives searching for that same old American song feeling, and subsequent loves disappoint. Boredom sets. With dissatisfied days of half-witted love. And a head of hair that turns to ash.

"You're always in a hurry to get somewhere," he said.

I'm usually in a hurry to leave. But he doesn't know that.

That morning, we dressed and walked to the neighborhood coffee shop. Hand in hand. Languidly and sluggish. Half-broken. Eyes, half-open. Pathetic, I thought. It was the first time we had actually done something together in the morning. A morning after a Saturday night at the neighborhood bar with the cow on the corner. That morning we walked to the coffee shop and sat at a small, white, rectangular table. He read the daily paper and smoked unfiltered cigarettes while I sat cross-legged on the bench. I sat and let my mind wander. My eyes darted from the paintings on the wall. To the people walking on the street. To the sounds of whole milk foaming in submission to a modern machine. Déjà vu, I thought. It reminded me of a café in Paris, and then I was comforted. The sun was shining that day in Paris. People walked quickly. Jesus wasn't preaching, and there was no distant television. I looked over.

I looked over to the clock on the wall. The clock on the wall above the modern machine told me time had passed. A relative issue. I had nowhere to be. But he did. He opened the door for me, cigarette still burning like a thorn in his side. A glimmer of consciousness in his eye. Back straight. Well-tuned. A newly caffeinated pose. He looked at me across the room. I got my coat on. A leopard-spotted one with a stranger's initials embroidered in the lining. C.M.T. I put on my coat and walked through the doorway.

We were walking on the sidewalk, a few feet apart. Languidly. I was conscious of it. We were walking on the sidewalk outside the neighborhood café. The one near the bar with the cow on the corner. Somewhere between the sidewalk and the street he called out my name. Between the sidewalk and the street, I heard a voice. Unfamiliar and obscure. Elongated. Warped. Between the sidewalk and the street, I heard a voice. My head was still a blur.

Just then my ankle gave out. I fell off the curb.

Paris. All I remembered was a painting on the wall. A cigarette burning beside me. A clock on a wall. The sounds of whole milk foaming. Another thorn in my side.

I fell off the curb and onto the street. Onto hardened tar. A black chasm. And sprained my ankle.

I fell off the curb and into a chasm. He called me a klutz and finished his sentence.

§ § §

I dreamt that I was at a warehouse party. I was asleep as I dreamt in a stranger's bed. My eyes were zigzagging under the shade of my eyelids. Left, then right. Then left again.

I dreamt that I was at a warehouse party. A costume party, actually. Everyone at the party was wearing masks. There, inside the warehouse, during the party, I lost my car. It was folded in a corner. In pieces. I was digging through some rubble, bottles of beer, clothes, dead furniture. Looking for all the pieces to my car.

And then I found them, the pieces to my broken car. My car was bright pink. Fuchsia. Plastic. In the shape of an old Volkswagen Bug. But tiny. About the size of a tricycle. Dressed in a leopard-spotted coat and my black heeled boots, I picked up the pieces of my car, and carried them out, over my head, like a trophy. Out of the party. Out of the place where people masqueraded in distorted faces. That weren't theirs. Out of the warehouse. And into the twilight.

§ § §

"Johnnie."

Time is entirely relative.

"Hey, babe."

Six hundred and thirty-eight suns had risen. Over the horizon. At intervals of 23 hours 56 minutes and 41 seconds. Give or take a second or two. Time had passed.

The Earth travels the same course to ensure we repeat ourselves daily. It parrots the rhyme without the reason.

One second.

I awoke one morning on the other side of town in a strange bed with a stranger lying next to me. His eyes, wide open, gazed at me lazily. As if they were trying to decipher how much time had passed and how to interpret this passage.

I awoke one morning in a strange bed. It had the same lumps. The same incline. The same corpse in the fetal position. My eyes, half-open, scanned the walls of the room. A photograph of parents in their youth. A dark picture of the sun reflected in sea. Postcards on the bed frame. A blue postcard. A woman. Where have I seen that image before?

"Morning." His voice sounded scratchy. Warm. Like a brandy and a slow cigarette.

I rolled over to the left and curled up in front of him. As he drew me in closer, he coveted me with his right arm. I looked over to the clock on the wall. It was half past the hour, the clock looked familiar. But his arm didn't feel that familiar. It weighed heavier, less yielding. Safer. More intentioned, perhaps.

"Breakfast, babe?" He had nowhere to be.

We dressed and walked arm in arm to his cream-colored Volkswagen Bug. I wore the last night's black vintage dress, tailored in the '50s, that exposed my knees, my calves. My ankles. He wore long jeans, a T-shirt, and black leather boots laced above the ankles. We walked together to his old Bug, with a dent in the fender the shape of a moon half-full. He opened the passenger door. And I crawled over the space where the passenger seat should have been, and into the backseat.

"What happened to the passenger seat, Johnnie?"

"That seat made my car drag. The shocks don't give and the right wheel scrapes against the dent in the fender." He sat in the driver's seat, lit an unfiltered cigarette, and shaded his eyes with sunglasses. Silver-rimmed with impenetrable lenses. He reached across the dash, and turned on the stereo.

I crawled into the backseat and stretched my legs across the empty space where the passenger seat should have been. In the distance I heard the sounds of scraping. Metal on metal. Velvet Underground on the stereo. Muffled by my meandering thoughts. Copper on steel. Bone on bone. Tendon on tendon. A muscle. A fall. Followed by a sentence I never did hear.

Cars rushed by. People crossed the streets when the lights changed their hues. A young girl waved out of the back window of an old Pontiac. Mommy are we there, yet? An old man crossed the street at a funeral pace, ambling the periphery of a very long time.

Johnnie took a drag of the white cigarette, and white smoke filled the inside of the cream-colored Bug, the one with a dent in the fender the shape of a moon half-full. Through the haze, street signs passed me by. White signs, and rectangular, with sequential numbers inscribed on their faces.

The car pulled over. Music faded, then died. Rectangular signs stationed. He squashed his cigarette in the ashtray. Overflowing.

The car pulled over, and he let me out of the backseat. We walked arm in arm across the street toward the café. Me, in my dress that exposed my knees. My calves. My ankles. He, in his black leather boots. We walked arm in arm toward the café. The one next to the shop with birds on the sidewalk. Outside the aviary shop, a blue parrot was perched on a pole. A blue parrot with long tail feathers in primary colors. Red. Yellow. And green. It was bobbing its head. We stood together in unison and watched the blue parrot bob its head up and down.

"I think that's a warring call. I think parrots bob their heads when they feel threatened or vulnerable. Don't they?" His voice sounded smooth and sleepy. Thoughtful perhaps. His head and hair turned to face me.

"I don't know, Johnnie. I don't know much about birds."

In the restaurant we sat on the patio at a small round table. The tablecloth was red. The umbrella was yellow. The sky, a murky blue. We sat and ate omelets with potatoes and corn bread. We ate slowly. Deliberately. As we talked about black holes and their dimensions. We were wondering if people would stop aging at the periphery of a black hole. And what would happen to the beat of a heart.

Give or take a second or two.

After we ate, he smoked unfiltered cigarettes. I sat cross-legged under the umbrella and watched droplets of water sweating from my water glass.

We left and paused at the aviary outside the café. The blue parrot was still perched on the pole. The blue parrot with tail feathers in primary colors. Red. Yellow. And green. Next to the blue parrot, a new red parrot was perched on the same pole. A red parrot with feathers in Red. Yellow. Green. We stopped to watch both of them. We stopped to watch the parrots as they bobbed their heads in unison.

Time had passed. A relative issue.

"Should I put the passenger seat back in the car?" We got into his cream-colored Volkswagen Bug, dented.

"I thought the shocks couldn't take it."

"I know. Remind me to get that fixed, babe."

§ § §

Bright colors and costumes and a clown sent me spinning. I dreamt I was looking for a seat in the bleachers of a circus show. Children screaming. Mothers scolding. "Get away from there!" The sounds of horns and lions roaring. I was walking around and around, looking for a seat. But there were no circus seats.

Then, I started climbing up a ladder to get a better view of the bleachers, still looking for a seat. I climbed higher and higher. Then higher and higher. Another platform. Another woman. Me, but not me. Not me decorating myself in a costume of red sequins and yellow feathers. I thought to myself, I don't remember ever being trained to walk the high wire. And if I was trained, how could I forget?

On the wire, I had a heavy pole ten feet long, teetering to the right, teetering to the left. Then I started walking, one foot in front of the other.

§ § §

As the planet Mercury revolves around the sun, it looks at first to travel in an oval orbit. But its orbit is not quite elliptical. It's oval-shaped, but slightly warped. So after each revolution around the sun, Mercury fails by a tiny bit to return to its starting point. It draws the portrait of petals around the seeds of a sunflower.

I awoke one morning in the same strange bed.

"Breakfast, babe?"

I looked over to the clock on the wall.

"Sure."

We dressed and walked hand in hand to his dented Volkswagen Bug. I sat in the backseat. Carried my bag of books. He carried his camera. An old silver Nikon with a strap in primary colors.

I sat in the backseat. "What ever happened to your shocks, Johnnie? Didn't you want to get them fixed so you can install the front seat?"

"I know. I'm just lazy." He sat in the driver's seat, lit an unfiltered cigarette, and shaded his eyes. Impenetrable.

He drove on a street lined with rectangular churches. As I sat in the backseat and watched people dressed in their Sunday best. Flowing dresses. Flowered hats. Sun rays. Petal-shaped.

He drove on a street lined with white rectangular churches to a diner I had never been to. We got out of the car and walked, hand in hand, to the entrance door. The diner was dark and hollow. Shaped like the belly of a great white whale, or Noah's ark. A cave in the middle of the desert. Where fish once swam, then died. Parched. And grew legs. The ocean is a fish's kidney. Once the fish swims ashore, it grows legs to walk and an internal kidney. So human kidneys are actually our reserve of ocean water. Without them, we would parch, and I thought, it's time I learned to swim.

We got out of the car and walked hand in hand to the entrance door. Unhinged our hands in the doorway. A few steps underground. We walked single file to reach the main floor. With the tables, the chairs. The tables were covered with yellow plastic tablecloths. The plastic tablecloths were covered by a sheet of glass. Porcelain vases. Fake flowers. We sat at the table under the window. Me with my back faced to the sun. He faced the sun. Johnnie. We sat at the plastic table. Perched on two vinyl chairs.

He photographed me. Snapped. A white-and-black negative of a black-and-white photograph. A silhouette of my image, the sun behind me. Rays emanating like in images of the virgin in stained glass churches.

I looked over the menu. Decided on a cheese omelet, hash browns, and wheat toast. Orange juice and coffee. He looked over the menu. Decided on a ham and cheese omelet, hash browns, sausages, and wheat toast. Orange juice and coffee. And we waited. As we sat perched on two vinyl chairs. On opposite sides of the table.

Time passed.

I sipped my coffee. My orange juice. And then I heard his voice.

"I'm going out with some old friends of mine tonight. And I would like for you to come. But only if you're going to have a good time." His voice sounded warped. Languid and crooked. Like an old record that was exposed to the sun. On a phonograph from long ago.

"But only if you're going to have a good time."

I looked over to the clock on the wall. Wondered if time was good. Or if time was bad. Quiet? Introspective, perhaps? Linear. Or circular. I wondered if time was the same shape as the sun.

The clock on the wall told me time had stationed.

The night before, I invited him out to a bar. The bar with the palm tree on the corner. I invited him out to a bar so that we could continue the conversation we had previously sparked. Like a match against the flint of a matchbox. A few days before. A few days before the night we went out, we were discussing the universe's relationship to the earth. The conversation ended abruptly. Over empty cigarettes boxes and dry wineglasses. So, the night before breakfast at Noah's ark, I invited him to the bar with the palm tree on the corner. So we could talk about the sun. The orbits of the planets. And their relationship to time.

"Do you want to go for a drink?" I had asked.

He agreed. Then, he invited his roommate Joe.

We spent the evening at the bar with the palm on the corner with his roommate Joe. Johnnie and Joe talked about their jobs. About their house. Their other roommate. While I sat quietly and let my mind wander. I was thinking about the universe and its petals. About the planets and their revolutions. About rotations. Old phonographs and warped records. How time must truly be oval and Mercury never travels the same path twice.

"Only if I am going to have a good time?" I asked.

The moon has two different sides, a light side and a dark side, depending on which side faces the sun. The ocean, too, has many different names, depending on the shore upon which it washes. But light and dark are one side. The seven oceans, one sea.

The night before, I sat quietly and let my mind wander.

"Yeah, babe. Only if you're going to have a good time."

I heard the hands of time slowing. To a halt. While a camera with a strap in primary colors took permanent negatives of my virgin image. Permanent negatives on black-and-white film. At the window in Noah's ark. Where rays of sunlight surrounded my mass of black curves.

§ § §

I awoke one morning from a cryptic dream in the same strange bed with the same stranger hearing the sounds of my voice saying, "Gooooo . . . aaaawaey." I was talking in my sleep. Warning my waking self.

The pendulum swung and swung.

"Gooooo . . . aaaawaey."

My voice sounded curved. Like the curvature of sound surrounding a black hole. A black hole where a star once shone, burned, and collapsed.

I was an adult in my childhood house. There were three of us gathered in the living room. My mother, my sister, and myself. We were casual in the living room.

Soon, my sister said goodnight and went to bed. It was night. Then, my mother said goodnight and went to bed. I got up to go to bed, but stopped at my mother's room to tell her something I had forgotten. Something trivial.

Something about the following day. An errand, perhaps?

My mother's bedroom door was slightly open. I walked in unannounced. There I found my father naked on the bed. He saw me and screamed, "You have no right to enter without knocking!" He stood and ran toward me with a wooden stick.

"Dad . . . I didn't even know you were in the house. I would have never entered this room had I known you were home. Dad, I didn't know you were home."

I awoke one morning from a cryptic dream. In the same strange bed, with the same stranger.

"Gooooo . . . aaaawaey."

§ § §

"I'll fight you to the death about this." His voice sounded dry and scratchy. Like the sounds of a meteor shooting through a desert cosmos. He squinted at me with small pupils. Like two sunspots against the backdrop of a blaze.

He was talking about blankets. I had been cocooning myself in his blue blankets all night. Protecting myself. From the cold. The damp. Keep myself warm and safe.

"I'll fight you to the death about this." They were joking words. They were fighting words. They were the first words I heard that morning. Then, my blue cocoon was cracked. Spread and disassembled. As I coiled and collapsed. Unshielded.

He lit a cigarette and walked to the kitchen to make a pot of coffee. As I lingered in a stranger's bed. Staring at the photographs on the wall. At postcards on the bed frame. A blue postcard. A woman. Where have I seen that image before? The pendulum swung me to the left, and I fell onto the beach of a cobalt sea. My silver car was being washed away by the tide. It was pulled to the middle of the sea, and there it was suspended on the surface. Floating like a buoy. A silver splash in the blue horizon.

In my dream I stood on the seashore, concerned about my car and wondering about the marine animals beneath the surface of the sea. The sea lions and sea snakes. Seal of Approval. Where does one get it? And when do we know we have it? Watching my island of man-made materials.

Then I wondered how I was going to get home.

I awoke and crawled out of the blue bed. Walked to the kitchen. Looked over and saw Johnnie at the wooden table near the window. Drinking coffee, eating a toasted bagel, reading the paper. Hungry, I looked in the toaster. The toaster was empty.

I stood at the counter and poured myself a cup of coffee. Milk followed. Then sugar. I took the spoon from the counter top, the spoon he had previously used, and stirred my coffee. I left the spoon in my coffee cup. And sat down on the couch and let my mind wander.

Time passed. He stood and walked to the counter and poured his second cup. Milk followed. Then sugar. He looked for the spoon on the counter to stir his coffee.

"Where'd you put the spoon, babe?"

"It's right here."

He walked over to the couch, walked over to where I was sitting, reached over to my coffee cup, and took the spoon.

"Now, that's a habit we've got to break," he said. Sincere. Insincere. They were joking words. They were fighting words.

"I've drank my coffee with a spoon in my coffee cup for 15 years. And I will always drink coffee with a spoon in my coffee cup." Definitely fighting words.

He took the spoon away from me. Laughed. Wrestled with me, playfully. Wrestled with me. And said, "Don't take everything so seriously." Then he kept the spoon.

"I'll fight you to the death about this."

He was talking about the blankets.

'Til death do us part.

§ § §

The pendulum swung me to the left and I dreamt I was flying in a blue-green sky. It was dusk. The sky covered me in crystals. Sapphire. Jade. The sky covered me in moss. Underwater.

Then I heard a door open and slam shut. Bags dropping. Strange footsteps in the hallway. I opened my eyes.

"Hey, babe."

Another year had passed.

"Hi, Johnnie."

Since the beginning of the beginning.

"Coffee?"

One year, but time is relative.

"Sure, Johnnie."

And I never learned to swim.

I dressed in my pinstriped dress from the night before. Black, with white stripes, in vertical lines, down my dress. Like roads on a highway where cars start and stop, rev their engines, and start again. I dressed in my pinstriped dress, while he sat in his black leather chair smoking a cigarette.

We walked on the sidewalk next to the street divided by double yellow lines. Yellow stripes that delineate which side is safe to drive on. Where to stop. And when to go.

The old man behind the counter of the coffee shop knew Johnnie.

"Mornin', Johnnie."

But he didn't know me.

The old man looked at me with ashy eyes and smiled a nicotine grin. His eyes told me Johnnie had been to that coffee shop a couple of times. Alone. Johnnie had only been to his coffee shop alone.

"Two coffees this mornin'?"

Two. One plus one is two.

"Yeah, Freddy, two."

The old man then reached into a drawer and retrieved a fistful of hard candy. Smooth-textured. Brightly colored. Round. He retrieved a fistful of candy, and offered them to me. I opened my palm. The palm with the line that starts and stops. And starts again. I opened my palm and accepted the candy. Smooth-textured. Brightly colored. Round. I held them. Like multicolored planets in the Milky Way of my palm. Rotating on their axes and revolving around the sun. Rotating and revolving at differing speeds. On Neptune, the average day is 16 Earth hours. On Uranus the average year is 84 Earth years.

Somebody once told me what that line meant. The line on my palm that starts and stops. And starts again. They told me how to predict the future. But that was some time ago.

§ § §

That mirror image, that parallel universe, or just my wandering brain. A dream.

I was a schoolteacher in an elementary school. I was blond with blue eyes. Teaching a large group of children in a classroom. I was teaching the alphabet, as they were repeating in unison . . .

"*a b c d e f g . . . h i j k l m n o p . . .*"

Then a loud noise. Someone broke into the classroom. It was a serial killer I had heard about in the news. With one swing of his arm, he sprayed the children with bullets. Blood splattered on the blackboard. On the tables. On the chairs and windows.

I knew I was next and thought, "The only way to escape death is to identify with the murderer." I grabbed his hand, pulled him toward me, and kissed him on the mouth. And then we left. Together, we left the children dead in their seats. Left the classroom. Left the school and the city. Left the country. Altogether.

I accompanied him on his shooting sprees. My newly found love. He trusted me. He was killing everyone he saw, and I was killing everyone he saw.

§ § §

I awoke one morning in my own bed. A thick red blanket. The smell of stale smoke. With the sounds of some song swimming through my brainwaves.

The pendulum swung me to the right as I heard the mechanical ring.

Gravity swung me to the left. I was dreaming of a song.

The pendulum swung me to the right as I heard the mechanical ring.

Gravity swung me to the left. About another Johnnie.

The pendulum swung me to the right as I heard a mechanical ring.

Gravity swung me. The phone was ringing. I opened my eyes and picked up the phone.

"Hello?" My voice, cracked.

"Breakfast, babe?" His voice, closed.

"Hi, Johnnie." Hi, Johnnie.

The phone stopped ringing. The song stopped singing. I rolled over, and over again. My ankle ached. My eyes, half-shut, stared at the clock on the wall. The hands were pointing to a different time. Different from right now. Different from forever.

"Breakfast, babe?"

The smell of burning trees.

"Sure. Where to?"

Go away.

"The café on Fourth Street by the aviary."

The smell of burning tar.

"The café on Fourth by the aviary."

The smell of burning hair. My hair.

I brushed my teeth. Washed my face with my bare hands. Dressed in my cotton vintage dress. Blue cotton with small white spheres.

The truth is, there are no perfect spheres.

The Earth is the third planet from the sun. Its shape is almost spherical, but it's flattened slightly at the poles. At the center of the Earth, there is a solid iron sphere surrounded by a sea of liquid iron. This solid iron sphere spins within the iron sea very much as the Earth spins in space. But, because of the difference in size, the core seems to spin faster than its home planet.

I dressed in my blue cotton dress with small white spheres. Flattened slightly at the top. Slightly at the bottom. I dressed and drove downtown in my silver splash floating on the sea. Toward the restaurant near the aviary shop. The sun eclipsed my view. I drove downtown and parked.

I crossed the street in my blue cotton dress with small flattened circles. And heard my name called. From across two double yellow lines. Then I turned my face to see the sun.

"It's closed."

"Closed? Why?"

"They're doing renovations."

"Renovations, huh. Where to now, Johnnie?"

"Let's go further downtown to the place next to the bar with the cow on the corner."

"Okay. Should I just meet you there?"

"Yeah, babe."

I crossed the street in my blue and white dress, got in my silver car, and drove further downtown and parked. Then I crossed a street with a different name, and walked on the sidewalk to meet the same crazy Johnnie.

The door was closed. The sign was large. It read, "Closed for renovations."

Across the street a building was being torn down. With two different stories. One significantly taller than the other. Half the building was erect. The other half lay dead on the side of the road. I looked over to the clock on the wall.

And was blinded by the sun in the sky.

Around the world, a pendulum swung.

Down the block, another street was under repair.

The smell of burning tar. A smoky stale stench. And halfway around the world, negotiations for peace were taking place, between two different leaders. With two different histories. Two different blood types.

A wall was built.

A wall surrendered.

Time.

"How about the diner down the street?"

"Okay, Johnnie."

This time we walked together. Unlinked and a few feet apart, to an open diner, for breakfast.

I lied behind a masquerade smile. I told him about my good night's sleep and my good night dreams. I had a good time the night before.

Is it my time to ask, Johnnie? Is it my imagination? Have I slipped? Have I fallen? Which way did I go?

I told him stories. Stories about my past, stories about my future, and how these stories link up with the present. I said things that didn't resonate with the truth in my center. I told him about waking and walking and moving myself in a linear direction toward myself.

Is it time for me to go?

I was spinning in the opposite direction. I couldn't catch up with the truth. I needed more time to think. To let my mind wander. To recalculate my dreams and discover a new equation. I wasn't ready. It wasn't time.

My center was warm. Exterior emblazed. Tar black. And inefficient.

I had run out of time.

With no place to run.

Then gravity caused my fall.

Off the curb and onto the street.

And Your Messages

read, They are starving us, or, They have cut off my ears, or, They have pierced my eyes, or, They have cut off my hands. And you wanted to cut off my hands. You told me the gangrene would set. And I was the woman who fingered her necklace, having admitted to having a dream. Then you cut off my hands and told me I couldn't vote for democracy. You said, Go to the olive tree. But I'd cut off my hands just to touch you. Shut my eyes with dull wire. Tear out my heart so you'd know how I feel. Because this is too big. You see it too clearly.

This is too big. God refused to save me. And when I steamed off the stamp, I found your hidden messages. And your messages read, They have plucked out my teeth, or, They have cut out my tongue, or, They cut off my cuffs and gave me a system. But your words were like blinds. So I asked you, Why I should love this body? And you said, Because it is lordly. And I said, Should I prove false or weaken in my determination, may the soldiers of the Pope cut off my hands and feet. So I cut off my hands and held them away and you said, Pull my hands and make them yours. So I pushed my dead hands against your dead chest in hopes that I could serve you. Trains slammed into one another. I tried to pull you out of the ditch, but the head is always the longest journey. My body is still forming. My hands are still haunting. And when you gagged my mouth, I sang through the holes of my eyes. I am yours only in the dark. And you cut off my hands, sealed my ears with wax, sewed my mouth closed, and made my cords two twisted voids. Toilet bowl finger tuck voice box chain gang. I am sorry for your infatuation. I am sorry that you failed at the jail. I am sorry that you carve the infinite shit. After all, the lost orchid isn't worth anything. So cut off my hands, rational man, and hang me from the gibbet upside down. The sky is all blown like a scrap of paper. Because this is too big. And I don't care if it is the next big thing.

The Muffles of Dolls

I admire it. It's like the common fountain whose silver drops flow out. Like the disease that spreads on government. Like the chance of a poisoned apple. Of a bullet in Russian roulette. Your corruption is the presumption of what you ought not do.

You still haunt me, ghost. You who wears a slighted towel for a slighted shirt. After the fashion of the mantles. Slighted, the same way blackbirds fatten in hard weather. Some say you were possessed by the devil. But I know that you have possessed the devil and made him yours.

Like plum trees that grow crooked over crooked pools, I hang on your ears, praying you to leave. I cannot rely on your advances and so spread myself miserably on my dependence. So, tell me. Are we expecting tomorrow? So, tell me. Are we expecting the century? There is a reward for me the same way there are rewards for hawks and for dogs. While you live with a kinder geometry. Soft in the unpinned future.

I hang fairly in a pair of slings. Your love is like a bed in a hospital. I sleep immoderately, lower and lower in the gallows. In a tent like a child of Israel. The goodness of my melancholy, a moth, hurt for the want of wearing, falling into the wayside war by way of gravity.

You tell me to laugh at your willy-nilly wit but I can laugh only at your fool, your small and wrinkled foot. Making faces, he fails to abide you where you sit. Head propped against the wall, like a mathematical instrument all out of true.

There's a duke, a perverse and turbulent duke. There's a deputy, a base, offensive deputy. There's a captain all full of wounds and a wife that endures the fighting. I will call upon you to take my fire. To fit me with the wrinkle of your mechanical wisdom.

I hang superficially from the leashes, worse off for the plot endured by Hercules. Honesty is all out of fashion, so we go on speaking in each other's tongues. Like men in suits, offended by the questions, entangled by the snares that feed.

Like men in suits climbing the stationary escalator. The upside-down elevator. Like men in suits who tuck their envelope ends inside their gross and welting belts. These, their second-best belts.

Stains. Time past. Darkness come to come. The invisible devil candies all of our sin. Great men with great lives live inside the cedar tree fastened at the root.

Scatter the tempest. Let these words be mine. Let my violence untwine the mountains. Like the flesh of the dead president equivocating in his passions.

This is the marriage of heaven and hell. This is the marriage of melancholy. Hear me chatter like a starling, flattering with progress. I am speaking of that deviled fruit divided by the steeple. That naked sword blushing in the unblue sky. That you would have begged me now. That you would have loved me so multiplied by the doubles.

I am that figure cut in alabaster wooing at the tomb. I am that widow with the spotted liver hanging fairly in a pair of slings. The hourglass gives a funeral sermon and we both end together. Diamonds pass through jeweler's nests, but will you listen? Hypocrisy makes the regular man walk crab-wise into marriage. Marriage is. I remember. My eyes are bloodshot for the wedding ring.

§ § §

You come from a painting. There is a rough cast to your plastic. You twirl the strings of your beard and set them in a sentence. Then you hum three or four times to recover your memory because it gives you good stomach to quarrel.

You become the merry president when you smile upon your prisoner hanging fallow in the gallows. So I will trick you into knowing me. I will trick you into giving me the lying thing, here in my dying.

Observe my meditation. If nature loves a lamb, a colt, a fawn, a fox, a bear, a toad, a goat, a swine, a wolf, or any limb, man stands amazed at his deformity. In our flesh, we bear diseases hidden richly inside our tissue. Then we regard the rotting body with delight and with fear. Terror is our best physician. Terror until we have no teeth.

See, I do understand your insides. My mind rides faster than a horse in gallop. So troubled is the mother so great with child.

Observe my meditation. Grafting is a pretty art. A bettering of nature. Tissues are encouraged to fuse and cultivate into newer buds. To grow an apple upon a crab. To grow a plum upon a leprechaun. To grow a boy inside a belly, cutting capers. The orange tree bears the greener fruit that blossoms as it swells.

I know the tricks of the false and rusty watch. And so, with a pistol, I search for cod. With a needle, I inject myself with salts of gold. I throw myself a stumble over my latent shoulder and reconstruct the piebald horse.

There's a poison in the halls of my hospital. A Spanish fig. Traitors are convenient for the sake of discovery. Safety is a false steward, a saucy slave. We pull it by the roots and bugger it into bigger bits. If I were superstitious, I would begin to count my accidents, one-one-thousand, two-one-thousand, but instead I take your order and make it flower, seeking shameful ways to avoid my shame.

I birth a son between the clocks. You take the accordion by the meridian and make the happy discovery of music. Mars is the human sign grafted to the Dragon's tail that man might strive to make glass malleable.

Like a tame elephant, you think I thank you, fingering the lute. My woe is your mirth, and you command me to speak lower. Speak lower. Then you hand me the handkerchief, and I wonder. Am I to cup the mother's wounds? Am I to eclipse my moony side? I may be thinking about my palsy or I may be thinking about my sister. I may be weeping. Here. Where the rhubarb grows upon the sponge.

§ § §

I birth another and then another and then I do implore. Let me but sleep. Let me fall inside the cage of your ribs, of candy sticks and sugar coats, I think I read this yesterday. This hospital is all haunted, but I read it only now. Let me but sleep inside your pocket, pestilent with intelligence. Let me grow into your ghost and wind my splintered tongue around your splintered heart. Like a splintered skein of unspilled silk. I swear I am in love. And laboring men count the hours most often.

I admire it. It's like the common flower whose disease flows out. It's like the chance of a rocket. Or the quicksand of clocks. Corruption is the presumption of what ought to become. Like men in suits who take to flying. Like men in suits who ignite the skies. These, the sidereal skies. Like the men in suits who parade these halls, tucking the envelope ends of my poly-cotton sheets. Like the men in suits who parade these walls, tucking the end of the body into bed. This, their second-best bed.

Venus has two soft doves. I read how Daphne is shaped into a bay tree. I read how syntax turns an empty foot into an empty fool frozen in the marble. How syntax turns high-flying airplanes into high-flying spades.

When I am married, I am shaped into an olive, an apricot, a fig, a plum, a peach, a pear, a pomegranate, a mulberry. I become the canopy over the tower of the stones. Articulate the word that paints the piebald sky. All of this is such vain poetry. So I look upon your face and say, now, tell me, now, what is it now? Then I plant my soul inside my ears and hear, Did you ever know a worser painter?

Pour your paper bullets into my paper bosom and fill it with your paper fire. Everything here is written to the spectacle. I'll earn my cicatrix. Then I'll keep to divers times. Inside my skin, I'll shine the reflection of greener fields. Because when I wax gray, I'll have the whole world in stitches. When I wax gray, I'll make my own stone bed and, there, you'll find me napping, having had the chance to loose my tongue.

The wolf howls. The screech owl. The rhubarb on the sponge prays lamely for the revolution. A brother wants you for business. A patriarch for politic. Small things draw small minds, like ashes to ashes, dust to dust.

The wolf howls. The screech owl. Dumber things like the paraquito. A salmon meets a dogfish who responds with some rough language. I live in the shallow river, silly for the smelt. See? I live in no deep valley near no great hill, and nature, here, is withering.

§ § §

The English mastiff grows fierce with tying, while the rabid tree, fiercer, swings the rope in mere ovals. You discern the shape of my adverse loveliness, my tears that are more perfect than my perfect smiles. With a finger on your cheek, you muse for hours about my silence. Then, you poison me with gilded pills as a comfort to your grace. You kiss my hand, then take the lights because the darkness suits me well.

You say that I am sick, and so I perceive that I am sick, like a mouse that takes lodging in a cat's inner ear. Like a loon, I sleep with my eyes open. Like the figure cut in alabaster. Like the reverend monument, made proper by the pity. The fool of the cruel physician. A box of wormseed. A salvatory mummy. My body is weaker than this, your paper prison.

Here is my hand. Take my hand. Let me take your hand. Give me the dead man's hand. Take my hand into the fire to warm you. Shake my hand for the reputation. Then, lead me by my hand toward this marriage bed and put the ring on my dead finger. Heaven has a hand in it. Hell presents our spectacle. And the otherwise curious artist slumbers by the small and fusty watch.

Take the dead man's dream fashioned out of wax and bury it in the dunghill under the lifeless tree, while I revive the more dead example of the loving wife by execution.

Despair, the stars shine still. Despair, this vain sorrow. You persuade the body on the bed to have its bones set in a new configuration. Then you persuade the fleshy lump to live long, live longer, only to be hanged from the beams of your impossible hospital.

I have a dream. A song is sung to a dismal tune. Doomsday fails at the date. Unfurls the world on fire. Hell makes a melancholy madhouse where the devil blows up my soul.

The greater doctor presents me with myriads of maddened men. Like men in suits collecting pulses. Like men in suits who bottle bootlegs of my blood. Like men in suits who siphon the body from the body. Making alums from my pee.

You tell me to run mad. Run mad. Then you drain the body from the body and sing lullabies through my eyeholes. You lead the bee to sting my hand, then you play me with your saxophone. This you do under my poly-cotton sheets. This you do with your poly-cotton reverence. Because you've already achieved that radiant soul, having already had the chance to chisel yourself into indifference, having already had the chance to distill yourself out of existence, while I still sleep with a litter of porcupines, puzzling over unspilled milk.

I have a dream about the dilated diamond. Let me explain. I grow fantastical in my bed because the wayside war disturbs my mind. A coffin. A cord. A bell. Here comes the executioner's wit. Here comes my more perfect peace.

This is the painted hour. Death awaits me with ten thousand doors hung from its geometrical hinges. So pull me now. Pull me more strongly for my lingering life. Pull all of heaven upside-down upon me. My body flies up and up so that your wolf can sleep inside my shadow. This is the dream that turns diamonds into pearls.

§ § §

The pedestrian asks if he can visit your patient. You give him a salary for his lust and instruct him, for better fall, for better falling, to dig the dead man up and throw the leg over the blunter shoulder.

See? Only eagles fly alone. Crows, jackdaws, and starlings all flock together. Look at what follows me in my pallid direction. Good gifts make for good ways make for more worser prisons. I hang fairly in from a pair of clouds.

I am studying art. Driving six big snails from this town to that town. Six big bulls I elect for president. Watch the wives in the wilting wings. An empty submarine shatters the stage. Why, the patientest man in the world must match me for experiment.

Let me saw off your beard. Let me your head, your hands, your inner ears. Let me fill your brows with brown civility. I see well with my oyster eyes. I see well that I could wind a fine fellow, a fathead, a sappyhead around my little finger. Never mind. You'll be more sorry when the whole thing dawns.

See, physicians are like kings. Wish the sick prince a small nobility. This is a brook of no contradiction. Forty days are filled with forty nights. Forty urinals with roses. To fetch or to frisk. To let him go. To let me think. So that I can speak. That I can love you in this, my misshaped shape.

You know me now that I am a blunter soldier. Now that my doors are fast. My kingdom come. So listen now. Restyle your memory of me after the rogues. Then follow me toward the blacker mass so that I may fashion my refashion.

Strangle all my children. See that they all get hanged. Tell my echo a pretty excuse. Like men in suits. The first fist argues folly. The second fist for revenge. I imagine it all. I imagine that I have committed the crime. Like the tied and the untied knot.

But I still haunt you, ghost. Here, inside your cubbyhole cabinet. Here, inside your hollow and dismal heart. The hourglass is singing a funeral elegy and all things end together. Seasons, diseases, punishments. So, I'll forgive your foolish poison. I'll forgive its fair and marble purpose.

I see, I see, I steal a diamond. I am quick with my more certain wishes. Quiet now. More quiet still. Watch the winter on my tongue now turn to spring.

Because I still haunt you, ghost. Tedious in your guilty garden. Tedious in your green sublimity. But I am hap. But I am happy. But I am happy, here, above the pinnacles, above the domes, above the spires. But I am happy here above the mountaintops. Above the clouds, above the stars. But I am happy, here, where I reside. But I am happy, here, above the height.

On Dissecting the Body & Lumber

The body is a wonderful thunder. Different from other machines in that there's no empty space. Built with deformity and packaged in a wrapper, everything here fits to perfection. So, work, for one, in total darkness. Revelations are no less astonishing for being so obvious. Violate the body before trying to understand it. Make space. Make light. Make pictures on the structures and functions. Collect the pictures in the large library, that weird repository for words. This is a seeing with the self-same eyes.

If the eyes are false, pluck them out. Stack them in infinite heights. Cut the body into four pieces, and separate into sections about the head, the neck and thorax, the abdomen and the pelvis, the thighs and knees, *et cetera*, represented by the black racks in the stacks. Mill the body rather than slicing it. Then pack it in a slurry of frozen alcohol. A rotary rasp. Ground the tissue. In the anatomically more complicated female, provide three to one. Ditto thrice.

It is like rock-hard diamond. It's like the grain of log. This is all curiously done by hand. But fat resembles nerve. Nerve resembles bone. And only someone who knows his eyes can tell twin from twin. The solution? Finer cuts.

How the Clouds Hung

when I heard, They're leeching me, and, They're extracting me, and, They're spackling me, but I was busy planting some seeds. It was large and it was dark and there were many people to avoid, and then they cut out my tongue. And when they cut out my tongue, you told me to sing those songs that articulate my dedication. And I walked into the hospital with my tongue in a box where nurses strapped, siphoned, and seized. Then the doctors said they wanted to cut out my tongue so I couldn't complain. Oh how the clouds. You held the door.

Someone remembered me to no one. Then there was the disaster that led me to the embrace. You cut off my hand to circumcise my heart so that my flesh, you said, may enter your temple. Everything you needed to know was inside me. Roots sprung from my mouth like barbed wire as wild streaks darkened the skies. But the sharpest of tongues cut their own throats first. So you cut out your tongue and asked me, Is this your desire? That I should cut out my eyes, more hammered than stubborn? That I should cut off my ears, more pelted than smashed? And if an angel should descend from the sky, let me not hold. The instrument is cold. The fire is dead. I want to confess. But even if I cut out my tongue a thousand times, I cannot hide my crimes. Oh how the clouds. So I cut out my eyes the better to see you. I cut off my ears the better to hear you. I cut out my tongue to call out your name. Get on with it. Cut out my tongue for it has offended. Close my mouth with your fisted indignation. Strike me with your hammer, your pummel, opinion. Nice weather we're having. You cut out my tongue and gouge out my eyes and boil me in oil and send me to hell. Because here lies my mind, and there lies the body of my mind dancing on the hatchets of your affection. So cut out my tongue and tear out my hair and cut off my limbs, but leave me to love. You were speaking in visions. No, you were speaking in tongues. I walked into the hospital with my tongue in a box and all at once the tumble of romance erupted and all went toxin and scramble. Then I reached for a new law that let buckets of rain fall on our streets. Because I see no profit in verbosity. Why, a single word unties a knot. So hold your head high. Speak brief. Speak low. Then cut out my tongue and gouge out my eyes and watch as our love turns to mud.

Double-Bolted Doors

A bellow that is not a bucket. A bucket that is not a bone. There is wisdom in slipping into oceans. Into those wider organs horning. The way churches slip into twilight. Stone after stone. See the plaything on the mantel. I lean toward the paintings. See the baby fastened on the mast. I lean toward the window. See the sea, see the ship, see the ship's low hull. See the winding of vowels by the function of the fist.

Ditto soliloquies fill your ears. All those twins in wigs disfigured. Wayward smiles on a wayward train. Ready for the runaway parade.

Ditto soliloquies by the bark of the brook. You, who have excavated my marrow, not poetically but with ambition, for your traditional obsession that hooks.

I feel like an ounce of water that underwater seeks another ounce. One ounce of ocean, underwater, landless, skyless, blank. Though I know that with my powers of concentration could bring me to build me a rowboat, singular in song, plural in wood. But I'm feeling a little wooden now, a little hollowed out. Like a reactionary door just opening and closing. While you live newly in your widening world, in a hugeness just beyond the horizon.

A fiend, a farce, a toady tale. Of passageways, of alleyways, agrarian fields and land. While I wend, I whisk, I row my boat. I, who never saw my father in all my life, floating on that fatal raft, that wrack of sea and scum. Wandering through my wandering illusions in search of winds that bind. Wanting to go home again. To break your merry bones again. To break the merry science of your brick-like trick.

I sing, I sting, I travel on. Without addition or subtraction, making hours double hours, making days those trebled weeks. By now, I hear, the dial strikes five, and prophecy like a parrot, peeps, beware the dog that barking barks, beware the dog that barking barks, with reason of the imagination being weak.

Am I myself? A mere anatomy, a mountebank, a threadbare juggler, and a fortune found. A needy hollow, a hollow tooth, and here my teeth that gnaws my bonds.

Am I myself? A mere anatomy, a mountebank, a threadbare juggler of a smaller fortune. You crack your horizon like you crack an egg to make my world a puddle. I recall nothing connectedly.

Of your ground, grow elm. On your elm, I'll vine. Listen now. To the spilt vile of whispering ink. From now on it's all open doorways. From now on, I'll coil myself eel-like. From now on, I'll only softly knock. From the inside out of your ship. There is a window that is not wide. And beyond it. A ship.

But your laughter sprinkles atilt. Sideways saddling down the rattling ground. So like a snow bank, a blank, I take it upon myself to signify a solution. I make myself a promise to liberate nothing. Doubled in the muck and impervious to time. Because this is the closest I can get to unhinging the chain-linked days.

Wrinkled echo on the wrinkle steps, I wander through my wound with metronomic accuracy. A gull-like mutt, prancing in the pantry. See me ripple with your apple eyes extinguishing all the windows. Take you a walk to get the hermit talking. For in the end, it's all never-ending. See here I, your outstretched memory, am trying to make a tongueless confession. With single words on which I turn. My mountain to the topaz past.

Because between boat and beam it was I who made a joke of it. Between aft and mast, it was I who made you weep. Between mast and scream, it was I who found the body. Face up and floating. Eyes doubled and frozen. Crowned like a small abduction and dunked between reefs. Don't you recall? It was I who found the body. My twin, my ditto, my go-ahead sidekick. Decked out and ready again for the runaway parade.

And in the end, it's all never-ending. In the end, it's all stones and doorways. These are the griefs unspeakable. So I lean toward the duller drone. Introverted and inorganic. Between buffer and bender, I make myself a promise to announce a more casual catastrophe next time round.

There is a body who drinks from the seaside sea. The way birds tongue their babes at dawn. Owls owl by the edges of nights. None the doubled to ditto.

There is a body. There is a body tragic in its muted past. Unhinging double's calypso.

Franchise

You skip that part. And we wait. She does not come. Then there's a question. Then another part and then from then on it's all stones and doorways. In the crux of any translated language there is always the next. A text. What did she say about yesterday? Yes. Something about a pigeon in a man's unfolded fist. It's something quite natural if the man doesn't wash his hands. But dirty. So. Yesterday a crippled bird and today a crimped sky but as always a question is a language tongue. The sun paints itself on windows, which look like your eyes, but never so directly. A verb drifts. Like all texts which tell themselves in time and not always toward an end. Something past. Something unreal. In a corner, a girl in sandals decides some interior thing. Not unlike the transparencies of strangers. Seeing through stories. You are a dream, you say. You are composing reality. Words miss each other as sandals flip in low air. In the shape of the range is another triangulated affair. She approaches. You remind yourself that this is a story. A thing invisible. Composite of conundrum and sun. Like dried glue. A glob. Globing dark. She approaches. I remind myself that this is a story. Told. You are a character. She wanders. Walks like walking. Caster of history. She has two ideas. One somnambulant. Another in tongue. Encroaches. Then disembowels the bramble. Can I . . . But that part doesn't suit her needs, so she skips it. You wonder whether the light, coming from franchise, settles well. There is something tangible. Then. She sleeps. You sleep. Presidents quote Jesus. Like walking she steps into whatever order justifies the need. Both of you order meals. The sun on the window would indicate the particulars, if you were aware. Awake. Meals arrive. Then the eating of body. Watch the pigeon's unbroken wing. The idea drops. The wine isn't very good. What did you say? I miss . . . The idea drops again. Is asking for a new one. And that reminds you. It's like when

Evenings

Bluebirds ballooned in some sapphirine sky as one aged told one youth stories of summer. Grandfather Time told stories, as Johnnie Blue listened with slumberland ears and waited for his girl, Lily.

"I remember when your grandmother and I. There was a barn. I used to. Took a man all."

Here, the moment therefore is written. What here opens, operas, limits, and situates, is hereby displayed and splaying.

"In this country. In our country. In my country. There was only one day at a time."

This time at last, what is being effected is the placement of quotation marks around the body. From this word "blue," we are doubling and multiplying and dividing, counted and discounted, concealed and concealing the unintelligible double bottom of this double-bolted door, sucking the vowels from the bunions of fruit.

While on the other side of the sliding glass doors, sapphirine sky turned lapis lazuli. Wild pupils so nighttime grew. As nighttime widened. And bluebirds circled the curves of the house, this country, our country, hunting for the eve's last cry.

And I because air. Because of something breathed in another language, repeated and resung, rehung and straightaway forgotten by the invisible. And I because air who hereby knows that the story must be triggered by the question of how many whenceforth times? By the question of how many whichway ways? More steadily, more dreadedly, than the otherwhich untriggered fist.

When out of the blue, a small crash sounded. *While voices returning like an endless recording. While* Johnnie Blue flinched, and Grandfather Time's eyebrows puzzled *this endless parading of earth and air.* In unison Blue and Time looked toward *this endless procession of glass* the sliding glass doors. Wandered toward the window doors, and dropped their doe eyes down to the ground.

While this way of sliding, of crashing, of breaking, of cramming together two lacks of a center.

And I because air. Because an ounce of air. Another pound. Bringing myself to singing. Bringing myself to song.

One of the birds had crashed into the glass. *And I because air. Because pushing, growing, because triggering a fear within fear, while all the while suffering a global distraction. A beginning beginning.* The bird lay belly-up and half full of death on the graveyard grass, spiritless and somber. *Splintered. Printed. Singed.* His bleaking beak bled red blood that spilled like ink in a small *and singeing* circumference, as he twitched in attempt to balloon *and I because air* as small birds do to fly away.

The dull ray gnawing, grafting directly through each organ, gluing forever to its own explosion, plugging pointedly into the outside of the inside-out of things. A black, thoughtless, dreamless retreating. A flowing out of the depths of tissue. And I, et cetera.

Then Blue asked Time, "Don't you think we should kill it?"

"I don't have a gun no more."

While feigning a frontal explosion under the false pretense of a present. Of the insistence and blue, of that deep blue is illegible outside a distributed chromatic organism of time. Blue passage of tenses into the twist of time through which the present and the future communicate their markings and darkling.

Evenings.

Moon then blushed to ruby red.

Evenings.

At what sort of angle? To what sort of projection? Until when are we living in a world where the possibilities of time are so ill-practiced, so ill-dreamed?

Blue and Time stood together, *the horizon framed*, behind the sliding glass doors beyond the graveyard grass, *while the checkerboard serving as a figure for the mime of time*, watching a bluebird stutter in apple red blood. And ballooning birds turned to rats as they flew round and round the night sky's cage. *And I because air.*

"I wish I had a gun."

I think. I am. I feel. I sing. I

Returned to their seats to retell tales, and wait for Johnnie Blue's girl, Lily.

find myself willing by the throw of the dice into the surrounding nothing, just as I enter into the blue form of my figure, without having foreseen what awaited me, without having opened up the possibility of their eyes.

"We used to have chickens." *While my palace has 50 doors.* "Where the swing set is." *While my parade has 60 drummers.* "Used to collect the eggs for break—" *While my palace has* Blue bewildered as Time's words unfolded *that spot indicated by the trace of sky* in distracted air.

"But when it came to evening time, it was your grandmother who used to wring their necks." *Folding and unfolding the roots of slight trees.* "Pick 'em up, right like that," Time said as he forced a fist and shook it in front of his own broad chest, "and then whip around like a lasso." *Scission. Like a scission.*

Outside, lapis lazuli turned onyx. *And I because there is just this.* Rats turned to bats and burst, and the ruby moon warbled a high song. *The scission one gets by leaping.* Then the branches of trees upsurged and stretched as if praying to a distant star. *The detonation in which the body is shot like a shell. Like a shell. Shrill.*

The bluebird flitted this way and that, in the small circle of apple blood. *While the blade of an apple red knife.*

"I wish I had a gun." *Teeth unclench in the darkness of a sewn-up mouth. While I find myself mutilated, wounded in my egg riddled with holes.*

Then, Lily. *Isolated but strong enough to go this way, to go on waiting for sleep.* "Hey, guys." *While waiting in this egg provoked by horror.* Lily stepped through the front door. *And there is the echo* "Hey, guys" *or rather the incision, severed, but still beating* She lay down her coat and keys, walked over to Johnnie, and gave him a peck on the cheek. *while the drumroll that covers the voice.* "What's going on?"

I, understanding the single murder of constant progress. She, rising, the laughing, the lips tensing, exposing the teeth, teething. I, again urging her to finish. My muscle showing my swollen head, while night erupting, turning, forming.

Johnnie Blue cleared his throat. "There's a dead bird outside, Lily." *Before what story setting a swarm of bees.* "It crashed into the window and fell."

Lily walked with light in her step over to the sliding glass doors and dropped her eyes down to the ground. "What are you talking about, Johnnie? Be more precise. That bird is not dead. That bird is very much alive." *Rotting, cleansing, burning, canceling.* "You should put that poor bird to rest." *The recoiling of firearms and possibilities.*

"We don't have a gun." *Of triggering.*

What stands at the very horizon of the world becomes this figure against the ground, taking shape as it faces, exposed and examinable, before her brow, before her mouth. Everything rising from the acceleration of sleep. The mirror and the extramirror, the implication of the error.

"There's other ways, Johnnie." *The scattering of stars while always the same fixed stars scurrying across the skydome. I, lying in the midst of night, echoing its cause. An empty cave. An empty jewel. An absence. Mirror-shadow-phantom whirling in a world of blue, the bloody knot of time, straining, lifting my head above the river, the cold vertiginousness of water and window, turning about my cage with change, against the multiplication of night engorging and the division before the law, before the law of her brow, before the law of her mouth.* "Why don't you just drown it?" *Living the law for this misapprehension.*

Blue and Time's eyes exchanged silences, as their heads bent to shelter their stomachs.

I, dying, come to life in a thought, a mark among marks.

While other suns revolving around a different arithmetic. Something counting inside me, adding myself to my own subtraction, without flute, without note, without voice already dead, the last note held for an infinity of time. Because I air. That last note whose vowels lined up and forever changed their places.

Lily walked over to the kitchen. *I, et cetera.* She opened one of the cabinets *The grass growing thick despite the pebbles* and retrieved a small, white bowl *I, seeing myself among myself* filling it in the sink with warm running water. *and the twigs. While the grass growing unalterably green* She walked over to the sliding glass doors and unlatched the lock. *with an obsessive quest for a way out.* She slid the *Minute, useless, obstinate* door *tireless composition of leveled sand* open with a silvery hiss. *The sky above darkening, darkening the avenues of sky and air.* She bent down to the bluebird bathed in apple blood in the onyx night. In the distance, a small star scattered.

"Hey, little guy." *All the while saying that this palace is furnished with 50 doors that open on all four sides, with their terraces, their domes, their gardens, their ceremonies. The sky still gleaming a nighttime widening.*

Wandering about over everything. Already exiting before the seed, darkening, while another day emptying in its blue-black ink, waking up singing and singeing like a bolt of lightning slipping, slipped, into a whirl of horns. I, air. Triggered in another language of repeating and forgetting and dormant.

She picked the bluebird up gently, *And from these four walls, the succession of mathematical proofs* cupped and cradled it in the shell of her hands. *that there is nothing here behind the insensible respiration* She carried it through the house turning red to the kitchen as blood collected in her palms. *these motionless fall of numbers, these columns of gold, time's ashes from a white fire.*

I, lodging in unfolding and deployment While silence boomed throughout the house. *like an opting for a past with the false face of a future made from figures not of the present, like a shooting through crosshatched waves of immensity, like swelling and extending, and finally, the square earth of the world,*

Onyx blackened while ruby reddened.

the dial's finite apparatus belonging forever to finite time.

Blue and Time watched with unwavering stares. *And to be sure, the principal arms of the house, the point of a circle, red in the gap as it never comes to be, unfolding its oscillations.*

Lily stroked the bluebird's belly, and plunged him into the small white bowl. *While oscillating,* The water turned to apple blood, *the world, worlding,* as the bluebird *encompassing,* expanded his wings, *the round dance like a figure four,* opened his beak, *in the case of content or concept, backwards on the edge* squeezed his *rootless* grasping *dizzying and looking backwards, needles, rods,* claws. Then stopped. *here, in the entrance of space.*

Blue and Time watched with unwavering stares, as branches collapsed in slow exhalation, as bluebirds ballooning turned red.

Swimming the Elephants

I climb to hear the replication of your sound open over concave shores. Draw my tears into the Tiber. To hear, tongue-tied in my guilt, the shriller melancholy music. When you say do, I do. Without standing on ceremony. When you say I am a dreamer, I beg. Let me dream.

From your eyes, I have no show of love. I turn my tumbled countenance upon myself. That I would see, myself, that which is not me. Vexed by neglect.

To turn myself toward myself but my eyes turn toward the outer shadows. Like no mirror that turns beads into pearls. Groaning under age's yoke, to disrobe the image. To drive away from vulgar dribbles. Trebled is a Tiber river, tiled, chafing. To bend the body toward nod. Wherever in Spain. That tongue of yours that drinks the tempers. The fault is not in the stars but in the wings of underlings.

In the here, in the after, I consider, I can hear you, in the after, I entreat you, in the present, I can see you, in the present, find the time, to hear high things. I'd rather be minced than weak in word.

In the here, in the after, I consider, I can hear you, in the after, I entreat you, in the present, I can see you, in the present, find the time, to hear high things. I'd rather be severed now.

But the games are all undone and you return, plucking feathers from your sleeve. In your infected ear, the niggling noises of the coroner and his whispers. I with chopped hands, lopped off and dropped, clap clap to open my coats, to offer my throats. You have stomach. So I dream of motes.

With lopped hands chopped I quake like a thing infirm. Climb the dank tree of my insolence. For fear of falling sicknesses. To come myself to know your heart.

Because the days are all tilting in numbers. Twilight curses duct upon my limbs. You call it the alchemy, but I know I sit low. You call it gold, but I bring forth the ladder that crowns. You call it heaven, but I know the crown that turns to clouds. Lowliness is my fitness. Base degree of my insistence.

Can I to myself? To cut off my head and hack the limbs like wrath in death and envy. To be the butcher that kills himself in his own unavailing shell. To strike the clock that strikes upon this ceremony. To call this twilight an unapparent prodigy of the unaccustomed terror.

Against your palace, a stony lion, growing, gazes. I cannot progress by the sidereal stars. I cannot retain by lottery. Like time's abuse that broke our idle beds.

To climb the ladder for loneliness is my lord. To lowliness is that ladder. Morning compass breaks upon the stone of slumber. To have no figure. To be that dank doll of the morning, renting, upsurging her rheumy, unpurged air. Don't you see? You make me half by visiting my sad heart. The art of which I at times number.

By rotation, I keep my eyes to soft molehills, soft like a toothless moon. Bloodier battles blow the world in flames. All framed up and ready to glow.

Because when I died there were no comets. When I died, there were no clocks. When I died, there were no wars, no histories, no whores. Horses neighed through windows. Lovers hooked their coats upon their backs. Ghosts shrieked in cuneiform streets, concealed in animated lionry.

You dream you see my sanguinary statue floating like a fountain with spouts. There you bathe your lavender hands. This doesn't apply to warnings or to portents but to relics. To my lowly crooked curtsy. My base and ample fawn.

You shake your bloody finger at the sky bedecked with sparks. Those spoking hands. These hazards of your faith that cursed light up my limbs, that let slip those dogs of war, that let loose upon the ladder, that let loose upon our three trees.

Now I climb the same tree to pluck my name from your heart. To finally get to the other side. The promised side. While hollow men like horses hoot. Flying off further fallow. I'd rather be decomposing.

Swells billow. Swims bark to bark. Glows glow a counter glow. Stealing buzz from the bumble bee.

Swims bellow. From arc to arc. The sweetest of sins wait in vain. Like your bulls that die happily. Like love. Like doves that fall to the ground and gorge.

Postscript

She woke up, said, "I gotta get coffee," and left. It was that way with her. She could be so distinct in her habit, her world, that each time she went for coffee she left a limb in his bed next to him. That was all he saw. An arm. Or a leg pressed against his hip or shoulder. To her she left a lasting impression of her heart. Or her heart itself as it lay there still beating. She was just taking her liver and lungs for coffee. It was morning. She had to go.

They became along this bisection. She drew a picture of him on her body. He spilled her name on his floor. They toured and renamed all of the horizons, writing moments under constellations of roses. And so they gained a little shape. "Look," she said. "It floats," she said. He said, "You lfet." But that shape became confusing to her. "Do you mean left, or felt?" she asked. And it would go this way, seen two ways from the same side, and vice versa.

They woke up, said, "Let's go get coffee," they said, "I hear the coffee's good on the island populated by emus and camels, and where the long-horned bull befriends the llama at night." And so they left. Or they felt like they left, anyway. For leaving and feeling were that way. They sipped coffee on land along odd rivers and banks. But as they faced only one another, each became the other's entirety. "The problem," they soon discovered, "is that the sea claims the land and vice versa."

"Don't go yet," he said.

"I cannot leave until I feel," she said. "Or is it the other way around?"

"Until it's gone," he said.

"Don't go," she said.

She woke up in the middle of the night, said, "These tenses are so filled with tension," and dismembered herself in his bed. He wrote backwards: On. On. While the nights became sawed in half, separated by two fisted blocks of sleep. He lingered in this gap, perplexed by the existence of cities he did not invent. She lingered in the laughter of another language, articulated in the personal present tense. Though not her own. Thus, impersonal.

She said, "I'm not present." He heard, "I'm not pregnant." And replied, "I, too, have never penetrated my own heart."

The trees outside him were stationary and looked like a painting. Inside, the city became mile-high and grew like a disease. He whispered, "This proximal distance. A city." While she tested her limbs to see which would float. In buckets full of water, she dunked her body parts. She said, "They're rotten." She said, "They're unripe." In the water, she saw not herself, not her limbs, but something she may have forgotten: No. No. Something *he* had forgotten. As left unspoken. Another tongue.

He woke up, said, "I know these tenses float and feel, but I know not what name you go. Goodbye," and left. It was the way he worked. He made casts of her and roped them from the stationary trees outside. She dangled from the branches imagining her reconstitution. "What shape of me will stay you?" she asked. But he couldn't feel her, for he was gone. Or he thought he was gone, anyway. For thinking and leaving were that way.

He woke up, said, "Hello," to her empty shoes at the foot of the bed.

She woke up, said, "How do you spell?"

He woke up, said, "L. F. E. T."

Waking became falling as this felling became them. She became both bucketed and hung. He became both tenses without a present. The trees were submerged by salty seas. And the cities became him. Distant. Underwater, she grew odd limbs on different parts of her body. And from her heart, another arm extended into the darkness and reached for things she couldn't name. She asked him, once, what names things went. He replied by building seven walls on a landlocked providence.

She woke up, said, "Come here. Come here."

He woke up, said, "Go away," and tossed a pedal boat out the window. Odd sounds were heard as the city slept.

ABOUT THE ART

The collages in this book are composed on pages torn from a book of poetry dated 1841 and have been created entirely by hand from a variety of sources. Each collage borrows its title from the piece to which it responds, with the exception of "Quake," which has been paired with "And Your Messages."

"Sorceress III" and "Sorceress IV" are featured opposite the contents page and title page, respectively.

Sandy Florian is the author *Telescope* (Action Books), *32 Pedals & 47 Stops* (Tarpaulin Sky Press), *The Tree of No* (Action Books), *On Wonderland & Waste*, and *Prelude to Air From Water* (Elixir Press). She has been awarded residencies at Caldera Arts, Stonehouse, and the Vermont Studio Center and literary prizes from Elixir Press, New Voices, and Brown University. She currently lives in San Francisco where she's an affiliate artist at the Headlands Center for the Arts. For more information, visit her site at boxingthecompass.blogspot.com.

Alexis Anne Mackenzie has exhibited her artwork across the United States, including solo shows in San Francisco, Chicago, and Los Angeles. She holds a B.F.A. from Tufts University/School of the Museum of Fine Arts, and her art has appeared in numerous magazines and books, including *Art for Obama* and *The Rest Is Up To You*. More of her art can be seen at www.alexisanne.com.

SIDEBROW BOOKS | www.sidebrow.net

SIDEBROW 01 ANTHOLOGY
A multi-threaded, collaborative narrative, featuring work by
65 writers of innovative poetry and prose
SB001 | ISBN: 0-9814975-0-0 | DECEMBER 2008

ON WONDERLAND & WASTE
Sandy Florian
Collages by Alexis Anne Mackenzie
SB002 | ISBN: 0-9814975-1-9 | APRIL 2010

SELENOGRAPHY
Joshua Marie Wilkinson
Polaroids by Tim Rutili
SB003 | ISBN: 0-9814975-2-7 | APRIL 2010

To order, and to view information on new and forthcoming titles,
visit www.sidebrow.net/books.